Hymn to the Range of Light:

Yosemite and High Sierra

Art Aeon

Art Aeon / *Hymn to the Range of Light: Yosemite and High Sierra*

ISBN: 9781990060076

Publisher: AEON PRESS, Halifax, Nova Scotia, Canada
E-mail: canaeonpress@gmail.com

Copyright holder: Art Aeon Works LLC

All rights reserved. No part of this publication may be reproduced, stored in a retrieval system, or transmitted, in any form or by any means, without the prior written permission of artaeon@artaeonworks.com.

An old version of this book was published in 2005 by AEON PRESS under the title:
In the Range of Light: Yosemite by **Art Aeon**.

<Revised: Feb 2025>

Books of Poetry by Art Aeon

Flowing with Seasons (2003)
Hymn to Shining Mountains: The Canadian Rockies (2004)
In the Range of Light: The Yosemite (2005)
Snowflakes on Old Pines (2006)
Prayer to Sea (2007)
Echoes from Times Past (2008)
Breathing in Dao [道] (2009)
The Final Day of Socrates (2010)
Beyond the Tragedies of Oedipus and Antigone (2011)
Dù Fǔ [杜 甫] *and a Pilgrim* (2012)
The Yosemite: Images and Echoes (2013)
Revealing Dream of Vergil (2014)
Homer and Odysseus (2017)
Socrates with Xantippe on his Last Day (2019)*
Tragic Comedies of Humans (2019)*
Du Fu [杜 甫] *with his Last Pilgrim* (2019)*
Virgil's Last Dream of Aeneas and Homer (2019)*
Following Homer's Odyssey (2020)*
Human Causes of the Trojan War (2020)*
Awakening to One's Conscience (2020)*
Dante's Sublime Poem of Light (2022)*
On the Nature of Humankind (2022)*
Cosmic Drama of Nature (2022)*
Tribute to Mentors and Friends (2023)*
Pilgrimage into Classics (2024)*
Simple Songs on Life in Nature (2024)*
Inner Voice *{2000-2007}: Simple Songs on Nature* (2024)*

*Distributed worldwide by Amazon.com as printed books
and by Google Play Books.com as electronic books.

Art Aeon

Hymn to the Range of Light

A selection of sixty simple, short poems, inspired by Yosemite and High Sierra: They sing of the magnificent vistas and the sublime spirituality of Yosemite Valley and the High Sierra mountains in California.

Dedicated to

John Muir (1938-1914) and everybody who admires the magnificent beauty of Yosemite and High Sierra and reveres the sublime spirit.

And

to the memory of my mother, Hahn Jong Sook (1917-1999), who deeply loved Yosemite Valley as a poet at heart.

List of Poems

{1} **In Sacred Haven**

{2} **Hiking**

{3} *El Capitan* **in Predawn**

{4} *El Capitan* **at Sunrise**

{5} *El Capitan* **at Noon**

{6} *El Capitan* **at Sunset**

{7} *Merced River*

{8} **In** *El Capitan Meadows*

{9} **Reflection of** *El Capitan*

{10} *Mountaineers*

{11} *The Yosemite Falls*

{12} **Music of** *the Yosemite Falls*

{13} *The Yosemite Falls* **in Mists**

{14} *The Yosemite Falls* **at Sunrise**

{15} *The Yosemite Falls* **in Winter**

{16} *The Yosemite Falls* **in Drought**

{17} **Glimpse of a Lynx**

{18} *Merced River* **in Drought**

{19} *Sentinel Rock*

{20} *Sentinel Rock* **at Sunset**

List of Poems

{21} *Sentinel Rock* at Dawn
{22} *Cathedral Rocks*
{23} **Autumn Reflection**
{24} *Yosemite Valley* in Winter
{25} *Mirror Lake*
{26} *Vernal Fall*
{27} *Nevada Fall*
{28} **Prayer beneath** *Bridal-veil Fall*
{29} **In the** *Bridal-veil Creek*
{30} *Cascade Creek*
{31} **View from** *Crane Flat*
{32} *Clouds Rest*
{33} *Hetch Hetchy*
{34} **John Muir** (1838-1914)
{35} *Glacial Polish* **in High Sierra**
{36} **Heroic Pines on** *Glacial Erratics*
{37} *Olmsted Point* at Sunset
{38} *Tenaya Lake*
{39} **In** *Tuolumne Meadow*
{40} *Mono Lake*

List of Poems

{41} Looking up Sequoia Trees
{42} Hallowed Tree Stump
{43} Touch of Eternity
{44} Jeffrey Pine on *Sentinel Dome*
{45} Meditation at Sunset
{46} *Yosemite Valley* at Night
{47} Hymning Stars
{48} *Half Dome* at Dawn
{49} *Half Dome* at Sunset
{50} *Half Dome* in Storm
{51} *Half Dome* at Moonrise
{52} *Half Dome* and *Merced River*
{53} *Yosemite Valley* in Thunderstorms
{54} In Memory of My Mother
{55} In Trance
{56} Prayer to *Half Dome*
{57} Musing
{58} Moonlit *El Capitan*
{59} Prayer to *Yosemite Falls*
{60} Communion

{1}

In Sacred Haven

How wondrous to muse
in the *Yosemite Valley*.
This sacred mountain-haven
is wide open to embrace
one's humble soul to find
who we are in nature.

Towering lofty peaks
inspire us sacred spirit,
pervading in awe and wonder.
Thundering waterfalls
invigorate our hearts
afresh pure through purgation.

This *Range of Light* is
imbued with sublime vistas
and numinous music.
An elated pilgrim prays
for inner awakening
in a deep, blissful trance.

Hiking

Fresh morning mists waft
along rugged mountain trails;
Climbing up and down
they lead to *Glacier Point*.

Dissipating dense fogs,
the glorious sun rises;
In breath-taking grandeur,
numinous sights unfold.

Soaring above the *Valley*
reposing deep in peace,
sunlit peaks of lofty mountains
sing in the blissful harmony:

Magnificent *El Capitan*,
heroic *Three Brothers*,
noble *North Dome*, and stately
Clouds Rest shine in splendours.

{2a}

Vibrant *Nevada Fall* explodes
in thrills; gentle *Vernal Fall* sings
with grace; the grand *Yosemite Falls*
exults in uplifting vigour.

Numinous *Half Dome* beams
heartfelt, compassionate smiles;
It looks aloof and mysterious,
and yet, so close and intimate.

Crisp, fresh mountain air
invigorates my body;
The wondrous panorama
inspirits my vision.

The lofty, sublime spirit
of the *Range of Light*
gently permeates
deep into my soul.

El Capitan in Predawn

This mysterious colossal figure
looms in the dim, subtle predawn light.

Thin mists veil lofty peaks,
towering aloft to touch heaven.

Ethereal beauty pervades
this serene *Range of Light*.

El Capitan at Sunrise

Resplendent rays of the rising sun
caress so tenderly the rugged,
stark and sheer cliffs
of this colossal granite massif.

It looks numinous
like a giant titan,
awakened afresh from a dream.

A paltry creature kneels to pray,
elated in awe, wonder, and thrill.

El Capitan at Noon

Magnificent *El Capitan* glows
in splendid, glorious sunlight.

It stands upright to uphold
the universal justice for all.

Its magnificent reflection
suffuses the limpid *Merced River*.

Blissful peace pervades
this abode of the sublime.

El Capitan at Sunset

This colossal granite-massif
is imbued with a deep golden hue
by the passionate setting sun.

It looks pensive, compassionate,
and magnanimous,
embracing all for protection.

A meek man bows to awe-inspiring
grandeur and sublime beauty
of gracious Mother Nature.

The *Merced River*

This gracious river of mercy
nurtures and sustains all creatures,
thriving in the lush *Yosemite Valley*.

Fresh snow-melt water flows,
turning, diverging, and merging
in exquisite, graceful gestures.

How delightful to hear
her jubilant, vibrant songs,
exulting in long journeys
to merge with distant seas!

In *El Capitan Meadows*

Beneath pensive *El Capitan,*
subtle mists veil peaceful meadows.

Lush forests of oak and pine trees
converse in an eloquent silence
something deep beyond my grasp.

Here, I relish the warm solitude;
Simple, heartfelt peace pervades
this empty mind in a blissful trance.

Reflection of *El Capitan*

Magnificent *El Capitan* soars
upside-down in a reflection,
suffused on a clear mountain stream.

A timid, elated face appears
on the limpid, tranquil water;
It looks deep into the inner reflection.

Mountaineers

Three climbers dare to scale
the colossal *El Capitan*:
Sheer, stark granite massifs,
rising aloft over three thousand feet.
They cling to a thin line of life
or death for taut challenges.

What a paltry, frail
creature human is.
Yet, why do we strive
to reach the summit?
I pray for their safety
in tense awe and sheer thrills.

The Yosemite Falls

Inspiriting grandeur
of the *Yosemite Falls*
makes me thunderstruck
in deep awe and wonder.

May this stunning vista
inspire me to see the sublime;
May the deep, vibrant voice
of nature resound in my heart.

Music of *the Yosemite Falls*

The Yosemite Falls in the spring-flush
exults in inspiring splendours:

Exuberant torrents explode
through sheer heights of steep rocky cliffs,
plummeting into stark chasms.

Deafening thunderous roars turn
into vibrant spiritual songs:

How subtly everything flows
in the mystic river of time;
All things merge into infinity.

The Yosemite Falls in Mists

Subtle mists tenderly caress
the mystic *Yosemite Falls;*
It looms aloft in the ethereal realm.
Here prevails the sublime voice.

Elated in a blissful trance,
a humble pilgrim prays;
May this mystic, deep voice
echo with his heartbeats.

The Yosemite Falls at Sunrise

In a blissful calm before sunrise,
I come to the vibrant, hallowed,
and inspiring *Yosemite Falls*.

How tranquil it feels here
amid such thunderous roars!
They sound like spiritual hymns,
pervading deep my elated heart.

In time, the glorious sun rises;
It shines vivid, resplendent rays
on the exuberant waterfall.

How wondrously they set ablaze
torrents of water splashing in awe!
Nature imbues this grand sanctum
with the spiritual exultation.

The Yosemite Falls in Winter

Sheer colossal cones
of lucid ice glitter
in resplendent rays
of the rising sun.

They adorn the lofty walls
of *the Yosemite Falls*,
exulting in winter's
awe-inspiring splendours.

Streams of melting ice
adorn the shining Falls;
They look like holy flowers
coming from heaven.

Ethereal rainbows
waft in cool, fresh mists.
An elated man bows
to the beauteous grandeur.

The Yosemite Falls in Drought

Dry, barren, mute *Yosemite Falls*
in searing summer's heat;

How eerie it feels to stand still
beneath these stark rocky walls.

Yet, I hear in this utter silence
its deep voice, singing in my heart.

Glimpse of a Lynx

How thrilling to peek
this rare, wonderful creature,
striding in graceful majesty
near the *Low Yosemite Fall!*

It disappeared quickly like a wind;
I wonder whether this is a real-life,
or I have been roaming carefree
in my fanciful daydreams.

Merced River in Drought

In late autumn, the *Merced River*
turns into a low, quiet rill.

Its deep bed, strewn with huge boulders,
reveals esoteric sculptures.

The exuberance of its spring-flush
is hushed to gentle modesty.

Everything flows with the seasons
in the mystic cycles of nature.

Sentinel Rock

The majestic twin peaks
of *Sentinel Rock* loom vigilant.

They watch over this pristine
Valley to stay secure in peace;

They guard all creatures,
nestled in this open sanctuary;

A lone wanderer finds a home here;
He reposes in their cosy bosom.

Sentinel Rock at **Sunset**

A serene alpenglow suffuses
vigilant *Sentinel Rock*.

Its subtle reflection quivers
on the gentle *Merced River*.

A strange little bird alights
on the calm, pristine shore.

It poises so still, as if painted
in a mythical picture.

Sentinel Rock at Dawn

In serene, pristine dawn,
sheer ethereal mists embrace
the stately *Sentinel Rock;*
It floats the dreamy *Valley* aloft.

It seems to ascend
into high heavens,
leaving us forlorn
in the mundane world.

Who will keep watching over
this wonderful sanctum,
when its sentinel flies
up into the beyond?

Cathedral Rocks

This grand and exquisite
sculpture by nature looks
to arise up to the high heavens.

It looks so lively with vital verve,
breathing out a mystic breath.

A pool of thawing snow
reflects the mystic light,
which beams from the sacred crag
deep into my elated heart.

Autumn Reflection

In colourful, ripe autumn,
the Merced River pauses still
at the foot of *Cathedral Rocks*.

The limpid water reflects
the ethereal work of art,
sculpted by ancient glaciers.

A paltry, fleeting creature
ponders at the grand drama
of nature in awe and wonder.

Yosemite Valley in Winter

Fresh, soft snow adorns
this serene haven.

Stately oaks and noble pines
shimmer in the muted winter sunset.

A herd of mule deer grazes
at shallow pools of melting snow.

A wanderer relishes alone
a blessed solitude in sacred mountains.

Mirror Lake

When I returned to *Mirror Lake*
in thirty years, sadly, it had turned
into a dull, desolate swamp:
Heart-breaking ravage of time.

The limpid, graceful lake has gone.
And yet, its timeless reflection
of the pristine light keeps glowing
on an inner lake in my mind.

Vernal Fall

Graceful *Vernal Fall*
greets a carefree hiker;
He climbs up on *Misty Trail,*
cleansed by sprinkles of rainbows.

Subtle moving pillars
of pure, holy water
gently purge and soothe
his heart with warm, motherly love.

Nevada Fall

Sheer, vast sprays of water
explode with exuberant thrills,
thundering aloud in majestic splendours.

How vibrantly they dance and sing
with such breath-taking verve,
inspiring us with uplifting vigour!

Prayer beneath *Bridal-veil Fall*

Gentle *Bridal-veil Fall* glows
in a serene golden sunset.
Its spray of holy water blesses
this peaceful haven for prayer.

The gracious voice of the fall
reverberates in my heart.
How gently it purges my soul
as the mother comforts her child.

In the *Bridal-veil Creek*

Crystal sparkling water sings,
cleansing worldly dust and rust
from my dull, numb mind.

May I immerse in pure,
pristine immanence
to lead a simple life in peace.

Cascade Creek

This clear, lively creek exults
at the fresh spring runoff.
Its vibrant songs resound
throughout the panoramic canyons.

A man stands still in a trance,
enchanted by its vibrant, cheerful sprays.
How gracefully they dance with such
invigorating verve to reach distant seas!

View from *Crane Flat*

Rain clouds are clearing.
Suddenly, *El Capitan* and *Half Dome*
loom in shy, hazy sunbeams.

They look numinous yet intimate
rapt in the deep meditation,
awakened in an enlightened realm.

Clouds Rest

Magnificent *Clouds Rest*
looms between *Half Dome*
and *El Capitan*.

It looks like a sacred temple,
where numinous spirits
gather for a divine council.

Floating subtle clouds
seem to guard its mystery
in the ever-changing vistas.

Hetch Hetchy

Once glorious *"Tuolumne Valley"*
has been condemned by man's greed
and vanity into this bland, artificial lake.

Let us repent our horrible misdeeds;
Restore its pristine, sublime beauty
to match with the *Yosemite Valley*.

John Muir (1838-1914)

Wherever I wander
in the *Range of Light,*
echoes of John Muir's voice
reverberate in my ears.

How earnestly he urges us
to appreciate and protect
the sublime magnificence
of these splendid mountains!

Glacial Polish in High Sierra

Massive, adamant, and vast granites,
polished by ancient glaciers
for countless seasons, look so
overwhelming and unearthly.

Yet noble pines make
their sacred home aloft here.
They overlook the magnificent mountains
in breathtaking, splendid solitude.

Heroic Pines on *Glacial Erratic*

Old noble pine trees triumph aloft
in heroic struggles for survival here.

Their entwined tortuous torsos
attest how bravely they've prevailed.

They've overcome countless severe trials
in this unearthly desolate terrain.

A pensive wanderer muses on
the sheer miracles in the journey of our life.

Olmsted Point at Sunset

On sheer stark, glacial erratic
at the desolate *Olmsted Point,*
a lone wanderer pauses
to pray in a serene sunset.

High Sierra mountains reflect
golden rays of the setting sun.
A gentle alpenglow suffuses
the lonesome figure on the rock.

A tranquil dusk deepens
in the peaceful *Valley.*
Subtle nostalgia touches
the wayfarer's yearning heart.

Tenaya Lake

Serene *Tenaya Lake* welcomes
a weary, lonesome pilgrim.

He reposes on its pleasant shore,
breathing in the pristine beauty.

The limpid, mirror-like lake reflects
stately peaks crowned with snow.

Here prevails ethereal tranquillity.
Time seems to take a timeless rest.

In *Tuolumne Meadow*

A vast sea of snow prevails
in late spring on *High Sierra*.
Distant mountains look like
tall ships sailing in the white sea.

Tuolumne Meadow cuddles
limpid ponds, fed by singing rills
of thawing snow. Strange wildflowers
bloom in exotic splendours.

Balmy breezes gently invigorate
my body and soul. Am I walking
in a waking dream? Or am I
awakened in a natural paradise?

Mono Lake

Descending the winding *Tioga Pass*,
I come across the surreal *Mono Lake*.

The vast expanse of still water
reposes in eerie tranquillity.

Exquisite tufa bedecks
the strange lake with exotic charm.

The more I look around, the deeper
I feel its entrancing magic spell.

Looking up Sequoia Trees

Giant sequoia trees
tower up to heavens:

The largest among all living
creatures on our planet Earth;

The oldest sage who has witnessed
the mysterious journey of our life;

The most magnificent, marvellous,
and sacred pinnacle of life!

Hallowed Tree Stump

A stump of ancient sequoia
stands still deep in *Tuolumne Grove*.

It had withstood countless harsh storms
and droughts through millennia
till struck down by a mighty lightning.

Elated with exciting wonders,
I enter the hallowed hollow trunk.

The timeless throb of a mystic life
resounds with a meek heartbeat
of this ephemeral pilgrim.

Touch of Eternity

Rapt in awe and wonder, I stroll
through the sacred *Mariposa Grove*:
The sanctum of giant sequoias.

These divine trees have prevailed here
for many thousands of years; they have
witnessed all the rises and falls
of the fleeting civilizations
in the mystic drama of humanity.

Trembling in humility,
I touch the lofty colossal trunks,
towering high to reach the heavens.

How gently their fresh barks caress
my humble hands, as if they were
to infuse a mysterious breath
of life deep into my heart.
Here, I feel a touch of eternity.

Jeffrey Pine on *Sentinel Dome*

On the lofty panoramic summit
of stately *Sentinel Dome,*
a lone dwarfed pine tree
has grown up from the stark granite.

It has prevailed here for centuries,
breathing in and out of numinous
spirit of this sublime *Range of Light.*

This impressive tree reminds me
of the thoughtful, righteous, and brave
Prometheus, who was bound to the crag
for teaching wild *Homo* to be sapient.

Meditation at Sunset

The sun sets in the mountains.
Calm dusk deepens in the *Valley*.
The mystic visage of *Half Dome*
glows in magnificence.

A pilgrim pauses by the river,
musing on inner reflection:
Vain thoughts vanish into the void;
All things inhere in immanence.

Yosemite Valley at **Night**

A still night deepens
in the peaceful *Valley*.
Towering peaks glitter
in limpid moonlight.
Beautiful stars flow
in the celestial rivers.

All creatures have nestled
in their sweet abodes.
Through tranquil hours, I stay awake,
listening to the vibrant song
of the *Yosemite Falls;*
How deep it resounds in my heart!

Hymning Stars

On this tranquil mountain night,
bright stars look to come down so close.

They hymn sublime music of the universe
in a deep, eloquent silence.

A humble man stays awake alone,
looking up at the shining stars in awe.

Half Dome at **Dawn**

In a subtle light of the pristine dawn,
a mirror-like pool of thawed snow
reflects the ethereal *Half Dome*.

The numinous mountain in mists
looks ascending to high heavens,
awakened in an enlightened realm.

Half Dome at Sunset

The pensive visage of *Half Dome*
is imbued with a calm alpenglow.
It rises alone at the golden sunset
aloft in the limpid azure sky.

Its serene reflection suffuses
the motherly *Merced River*,
gently flowing through lush meadows
in this pristine realm of pure lights.

Half Dome in Storms

In quick, abrupt thunderstorms,
ominous dark clouds shroud
Half Dome in tense struggles
of rapidly changing lights and shades.

Flashes of lightning blaze its head;
Roars of thunders thrash sheer cliffs.
A downpour of heavy rain drenches
a helpless wanderer caught by surprise.

Suddenly, it clears; *Half Dome* beams
subtle smiles in the stately composure.
The astounded man wonders at
the awe-inspiring drama of nature.

Half Dome at Moonrise

Dispersing subtle veils of mists,
the full moon rises above *Half Dome*.
Its mysterious visage glows
with an inspiring spiritual light.

Serene *Merced River* reflects
the stupendous, ethereal vista.
A mystic breath of the sublime
pervades this sacred sphere of light.

Half Dome and *the Merced River*

Magnificent *Half Dome* looks over
the graceful, serene *Merced River*.
She reflects on his sublime visage
in the splendour of deep, ripe autumn.

What do they confide to each other
with such ineffable expressions
of their deep, intimate feelings
in the eloquent, esoteric silence?

Yosemite Valley in **Thunderstorms**

In sudden thunderstorms,
impressive mists creep
on sheer granite spires.
Lofty peaks disappear
and reappear in ever-
changing panorama.
The mountains look floating
on an ethereal sea of clouds.

Suddenly, golden sunbeams
pierce through dark clouds.
They shine on stark peaks
soaring up to the sky.
These real mountains become
truly surreal entities.
Amid this sheer splendour
of mystic lights and shades,
all things seem to transcend
into spiritual beings.

In Memory of My Mother

I come to pray beneath Bridal-veil Fall
in the cherished memory of my mother.
The gentle, ethereal spray of the waterfall
sings for me like a compassionate mother,
comforting and blessing a forlorn child.

My mother loved to visit here and pray.
This was her sacred sanctum in this world.
She was so happy and thankful to behold
this warm-hearted, motherly waterfall,
blessing us to purify our meek souls.

In a Trance

Half Dome muses at dawn,
awakened for meditation
in the ethereal, numinous realm.

A paltry man prays
to see the spiritual light,
elated in a deep trance.

Prayer to *Half Dome*

In tranquil, pristine dawn
the ethereal *Half Dome* looms aloft
like a god rapt in deep thoughts.

It seems to know all things:
Past, here and now, and yet to come;
Our joys and woes, hopes and despairs.

A fleeting shade of man prays
to the sacred mountain
for inner awakening.

Musing

Mystic lights and divine music
of these sublime sacred mountains
inspirit my meek, humble heart.

May I breathe in their lofty spirit
to sing of the sublime beauty
and profound mystery of nature.

Moonlit *El Capitan*

Magnificent *El Capitan*
glitters in limpid moonlight.
It towers to uphold the heavens
and earth like the mighty *Atlas*.

The gracious *Merced River* prays
beneath the colossal titan.
She implores the god for mercy
to all creatures in the world.

A pensive pilgrim stays awake
through this moonlit mountain night.
He ponders how to fulfil
his vows before he falls asleep.

Prayer to *Yosemite Falls*

The waterfalls resound
in my inner realm.
They pour sacred water
to purify my soul.

Amid perpetual thunders,
deep, silence prevails.
In ever-changing flows,
utter stillness inheres.

Let this life flow freely
in the river of time,
as water flows lowly
to merge into the vast sea.

May simple songs of life
spring up deep from my soul;
May they gently flow forever
from hearts to hearts in love.

Communion

Humbly kneeling by the motherly
Merced River, a pilgrim prays
to the numinous sacred mountains
for awakening in immanence.

Vivid ethereal reflection
of their spiritual lights suffuses
the gracious river of mercy,
singing in the eloquent silence:

"Neither measure space nor count time:
 You are in them; they in your mind.
All things inhere in each other.
Flow freely into eternity."

www.ingramcontent.com/pod-product-compliance
Lightning Source LLC
Chambersburg PA
CBHW031420040426
42444CB00005B/653